The Fishing Trip

Story by
Mandi Rathbone
and Michele Gordon

Illustrations by
Julia Crouth

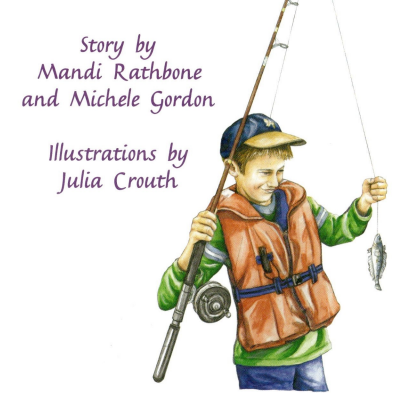

Daniel woke up suddenly.
He could hear someone talking to him!

"Get dressed quickly," said his father.
"It's a fine day and the tide's right."

"Great — we're going fishing!"
said Daniel.

"Hurry up," said Dad,
"because Ella's nearly ready."

Ella was Daniel's cousin,
and she often visited in the summer.
She enjoyed going fishing
as much as Daniel did.

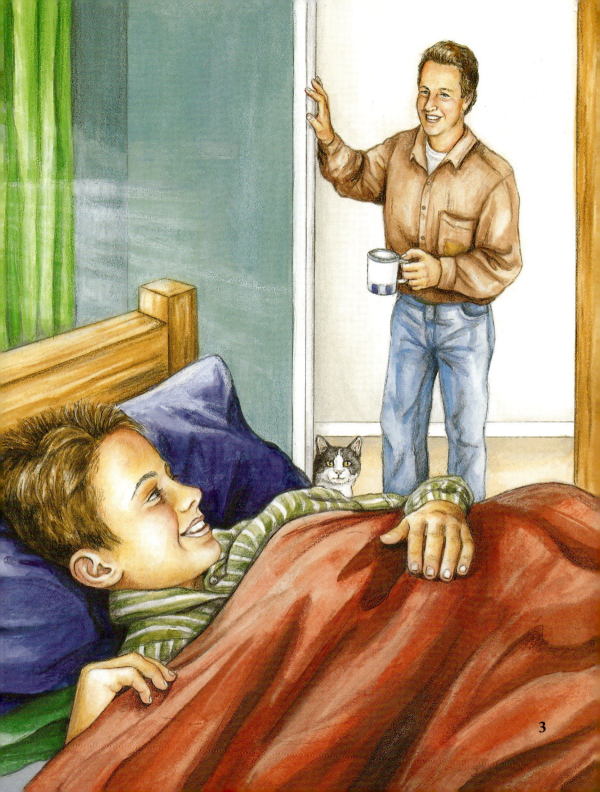

"I'm going to catch the biggest fish today,"
said Ella, as Daniel came into the kitchen.

"No chance!" laughed Daniel.
"I'm the fishing champ in this family."

Then Dad said,
"We're taking two extra people with us today:
Mr. Moore, who works with me,
and his daughter, Sophie.
Sophie is the same age as you."

Daniel and Ella looked at each other.
They weren't sure that they wanted
to go fishing
with people they didn't know.

"Sophie has wanted to go on a boat
for a long time," said Dad.
"But she's probably going to need some help,
because she is blind."

When they arrived at the boat ramp,
they saw Sophie and her father
waiting for them.

Dad introduced everybody,
and they all put on their life jackets.

The children stood back
while the men launched the boat,
and then Ella and Daniel climbed in.

Although her father was helping her,
Sophie looked anxious
whenever the boat rocked.
Ella wondered how she would manage
for the rest of the trip.

Sophie held her father's hand,
and felt her way toward the seat.
The boat rocked again,
and she almost lost her balance.

As Daniel watched Sophie,
he began to realize
how difficult it must be for her.

"The boat rocks when we move around,"
Daniel explained to Sophie.
"It will happen again when my dad gets in."

Ella moved the bucket, and said,
"The seat's right beside you, Sophie."

Sophie smiled as she sat down.
"I can feel the water moving
underneath the boat," she said.
"It's exciting! It feels quite different
from being in a car."

"Wait until we get going," said Ella.
"It will be even more exciting then!"

Dad took them across the harbor
to his favorite fishing place.

"If you pass me the lines, Daniel," said Dad,
"I'll start baiting the hooks."

Sophie ran her hands over one of the rods,
and felt the reel.
Then her father showed her
how to let the line out
and wind it back in again.

One by one,
they dropped their lines into the water
and waited for the fish to bite.

The time went by very slowly.
Nobody was getting even a nibble.

After a while, Daniel said,
"This is kind of boring.
Can we try another place, Dad?"

Just then Ella cried out,
"I've caught a fish at last!"

But as she wound her line in,
the fish slipped off the hook.
"Oh, no!" she groaned. "It got away!"

Suddenly, Daniel yelled,
"I've got one now!"
and he wound his line in
as quickly as he could.

But the fish was very small.

Ella grinned and said,
"You know what you have to do, Daniel."

"What's wrong?" asked Sophie.

"Daniel thinks he's the fishing champ,
but he's only caught a little one,"
giggled Ella.

"And it's too small to keep," moaned Daniel,
"so I'll have to throw it back."

They all sat and waited again.

Then Sophie shouted,
"I think a fish is pulling on my line.
I can feel it!"

"Hold on tightly," said Ella,
"because your rod's bending right over.
You must have caught a big one!"

Sophie yelled, "It must be a big one —
it's pulling really hard!"

Daniel said, "Wind some of your line in,
and then let it run back out a little way.
You have to keep doing that."

Soon they could see the fish
flapping near the surface of the water.

Sophie's father said, "You're doing well.
Keep winding it in slowly,
and I'll let you know when it's close enough
for me to scoop into the net."

"Here it comes," shouted Daniel.

"It's a huge one, Sophie," said Ella,
"so you're the fishing champ now!"

Daniel and Ella felt sorry
that Sophie couldn't see her fish.
Then they noticed
that she was moving her hands over it
to get an idea of its size and shape.

"My fish feels big enough for all of us
to have for dinner tonight," laughed Sophie.
"Thanks for taking me out in your boat.
I've had a great time."